Francis Frith's
Around Swansea

Photographic Memories

Francis Frith's
Around Swansea

Tony Cornish

FRITH
BOOK Co

First published in the United Kingdom in 2000 by
Frith Book Company Ltd

Hardback Edition
ISBN 1-85937-287-2

Paperback Edition
ISBN 1-85937-167-1

British Library Cataloguing in Publication Data

Around Swansea
Tony Cornish

Frith Book Company Ltd
Frith's Barn, Teffont,
Salisbury, Wiltshire SP3 5QP
Tel: +44 (0) 1722 716 376
Email: info@frithbook.co.uk
www.frithbook.co.uk

Printed and bound in Great Britain

Contents

Francis Frith: *Victorian Pioneer*

FRANCIS FRITH, Victorian founder of the world-famous photographic archive, was a complex and multitudinous man. A devout Quaker and a highly successful Victorian businessman, he was both philosophic by nature and pioneering in outlook.

By 1855 Francis Frith had already established a wholesale grocery business in Liverpool, and sold it for the astonishing sum of £200,000, which is the equivalent today of over £15,000,000. Now a multi-millionaire, he was able to indulge his passion for travel. As a child he had pored over travel books written by early explorers, and his fancy and imagination had been stirred by family holidays to the sublime mountain regions of Wales and Scotland. 'What a land of spirit-stirring and enriching scenes and places!' he had written. He was to return to these scenes of grandeur in later years to 'recapture the thousands of vivid and tender memories', but with a different purpose. Now in his thirties, and captivated by the new science of photography, Frith set out on a series of

pioneering journeys to the Nile regions that occupied him from 1856 until 1860.

Intrigue and Adventure

He took with him on his travels a specially-designed wicker carriage that acted as both dark-room and sleeping chamber. These far-flung journeys were packed with intrigue and adventure. In his life story, written when he was sixty-three, Frith tells of being held captive by bandits, and of fighting 'an awful midnight battle to the very point of surrender with a deadly pack of hungry, wild dogs'. Sporting flowing Arab costume, Frith arrived at Akaba by camel seventy years before Lawrence, where he encountered 'desert princes and rival sheikhs, blazing with jewel-hilted swords'.

During these extraordinary adventures he was assiduously exploring the desert regions bordering the Nile and patiently recording the antiquities and peoples with his camera. He was the first photographer to venture beyond the sixth cataract. Africa was still the mysterious 'Dark Continent', and Stanley and Livingstone's historic meeting was a decade into the future. The conditions for picture taking confound belief. He laboured for hours in his wicker dark-room in the sweltering heat of the desert, while the volatile chemicals fizzed dangerously in their trays. Often he was forced to work in remote tombs and caves where conditions were cooler. Back in London he exhibited his photographs and was 'rapturously cheered' by members of the Royal Society. His reputation as a photographer was made overnight. An eminent modern historian has likened their impact on the population of the time to that on our own generation of the first photographs taken on the surface of the moon.

Venture of a Life-Time

Characteristically, Frith quickly spotted the opportunity to create a new business as a specialist publisher of photographs. He lived in an era of immense and sometimes violent change. For the poor in the early part of Victoria's reign work was a drudge and the hours long, and people had precious little free time to enjoy themselves. Most had no transport other than a cart or gig at their disposal, and had not travelled far beyond the

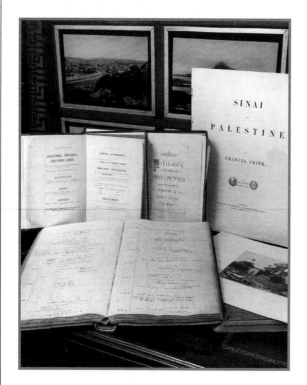

boundaries of their own town or village. However, by the 1870s, the railways had threaded their way across the country, and Bank Holidays and half-day Saturdays had been made obligatory by Act of Parliament. All of a sudden the ordinary working man and his family were able to enjoy days out and see a little more of the world.

With characteristic business acumen, Francis Frith foresaw that these new tourists would enjoy having souvenirs to commemorate their days out. In 1860 he married Mary Ann Rosling and set out with the intention of photographing every city, town and village in Britain. For the next thirty years he travelled the country by train and by pony and trap, producing fine photographs of seaside resorts and beauty spots that were keenly bought by millions of Victorians. These prints were painstakingly pasted into family albums and pored over during the dark nights of winter, rekindling precious memories of summer excursions.

The Rise of Frith & Co

Frith's studio was soon supplying retail shops all over the country. To meet the demand he gathered about him a small team of photographers, and published the work of independent artist-photographers of the calibre of Roger Fenton and Francis Bedford. In order to gain some understanding of the scale of Frith's business one only has to look at the catalogue issued by Frith & Co in 1886: it runs to some 670 pages, listing not only many thousands of views of the British Isles but also many photographs of most European countries, and China, Japan, the USA and

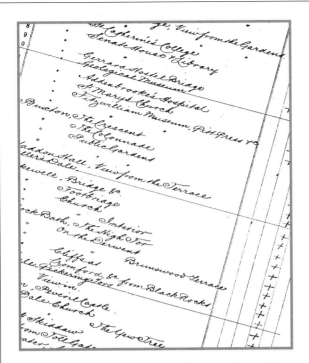

Canada – note the sample page shown above from the hand-written *Frith & Co* ledgers detailing pictures taken. By 1890 Frith had created the greatest specialist photographic publishing company in the world, with over 2,000 outlets – more than the combined number that Boots and W H Smith have today! The picture on the right shows the *Frith & Co* display board at Ingleton in the Yorkshire Dales. Beautifully constructed with mahogany frame and gilt inserts, it could display up to a dozen local scenes.

Postcard Bonanza

The ever-popular holiday postcard we know today took many years to develop. In 1870 the Post Office issued the first plain cards, with a pre-printed stamp on one face. In 1894 they allowed other publishers' cards to be sent through the mail with an attached adhesive halfpenny stamp. Demand grew rapidly, and in

1895 a new size of postcard was permitted called the court card, but there was little room for illustration. In 1899, a year after Frith's death, a new card measuring 5.5 x 3.5 inches became the standard format, but it was not until 1902 that the divided back came into being, with address and message on one face and a full-size illustration on the other. *Frith & Co* were in the vanguard of postcard development, and Frith's sons Eustace and Cyril continued their father's monumental task, expanding the number of views offered to the public and recording more and more places in Britain, as the coasts and countryside were opened up to mass travel.

Francis Frith died in 1898 at his villa in Cannes, his great project still growing. The archive he created continued in business for another seventy years. By 1970 it contained over a third of a million pictures of 7,000 cities, towns and villages. The massive photographic record Frith has left to us stands as a living monument to a special and very remarkable man.

Frith's Archive: *A Unique Legacy*

FRANCIS FRITH'S legacy to us today is of immense significance and value, for the magnificent archive of evocative photographs he created provides a unique record of change in 7,000 cities, towns and villages throughout Britain over a century and more. Frith and his fellow studio photographers revisited locations many times down the years to update their views, compiling for us an enthralling and colourful pageant of British life and character.

We tend to think of Frith's sepia views of Britain as nostalgic, for most of us use them to conjure up memories of places in our own lives with which we have family associations. It often makes us forget that to Francis Frith they were records of daily life as it was actually being lived in the cities, towns and villages of his day. The Victorian age was one of great and often bewildering change for ordinary people, and though the pictures evoke an impression of slower times, life was as busy and hectic as it is today.

We are fortunate that Frith was a photographer of the people, dedicated to recording the minutiae of everyday life. For it is this sheer wealth of visual data, the painstaking chronicle of changes in dress, transport, street layouts, buildings, housing, engineering and landscape that captivates us so much today. His remarkable images offer us a powerful link with the past and with the lives of our ancestors.

Today's Technology

Computers have now made it possible for Frith's many thousands of images to be accessed almost instantly. In the Frith archive today, each photograph is carefully 'digitised' then stored on a CD Rom. Frith archivists can locate a single photograph amongst thousands within seconds. Views can be catalogued and sorted under a variety of categories of place and content to the immediate benefit of researchers.

Inexpensive reference prints can be created for them at the touch of a mouse button, and a wide range of books and other printed materials assembled and published for a wider, more general readership - in the next twelve months over a hundred Frith local history titles will be published! The day-to-day workings of the archive are very different from how they were in Francis Frith's time: imagine the herculean task of sorting through eleven tons of glass negatives as Frith had to do to locate a particular

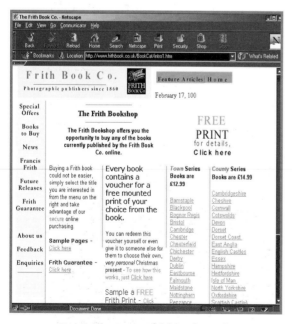

See Frith at www. frithbook.co.uk

sequence of pictures! Yet the archive still prides itself on maintaining the same high standards of excellence laid down by Francis Frith, including the painstaking cataloguing and indexing of every view.

It is curious to reflect on how the internet now allows researchers in America and elsewhere greater instant access to the archive than Frith himself ever enjoyed. Many thousands of individual views can be called up on screen within seconds on one of the Frith internet sites, enabling people living continents away to revisit the streets of their ancestral home town, or view places in Britain where they have enjoyed holidays. Many overseas researchers welcome the chance to view special theme selections, such as transport, sports, costume and ancient monuments.

We are certain that Francis Frith would have heartily approved of these modern developments in imaging techniques, for he himself was always working at the very limits of Victorian photographic technology.

The Value of the Archive Today

Because of the benefits brought by the computer, Frith's images are increasingly studied by social historians, by researchers into genealogy and ancestory, by architects, town planners, and by teachers and schoolchildren involved in local history projects.

In addition, the archive offers every one of us an opportunity to examine the places where we and our families have lived and worked down the years. Highly successful in Frith's own era, the archive is now, a century and more on, entering a new phase of popularity.

The Past in Tune with the Future

Historians consider the Francis Frith Collection to be of prime national importance. It is the only archive of its kind remaining in private ownership and has been valued at a million pounds. However, this figure is now rapidly increasing as digital technology enables more and more people around the world to enjoy its benefits.

Francis Frith's archive is now housed in an historic timber barn in the beautiful village of Teffont in Wiltshire. Its founder would not recognize the archive office as it is today. In place of the many thousands of dusty boxes containing glass plate negatives and an all-pervading odour of photographic chemicals, there are now ranks of computer screens. He would be amazed to watch his images travelling round the world at unimaginable speeds through network and internet lines.

The archive's future is both bright and exciting. Francis Frith, with his unshakeable belief in making photographs available to the greatest number of people, would undoubtedly approve of what is being done today with his lifetime's work. His photographs, depicting our shared past, are now bringing pleasure and enlightenment to millions around the world a century and more after his death.

Swansea - *Abertawe*

'And I went up, through the white Grove, into Cwmdonkin Park, the snow still sailing ... in the suddenly gentle wind. Dusk was folding around, like another darker snow. Soon the bell would ring for the closing of the gates, though the Park was empty. The park-keeper walked by the reservoir, where swans had glided, on his white rounds. I walked by his side and asked him my questions, up the swathed drives past buried beds and loaded utterly still furred and birdless trees towards the last gate. He said:

'Oh yes, yes. I knew him well. He used to climb the reservoir railings and pelt the old swans.

Run like a billy-goat over the grass you should keep off of. Cut branches off the trees. Carve words on the benches. Pull up most of the rockery, go snip through the dahlias. Fight in the bandstand. Climb the elms and moon up the top like an owl. Oh yes, I knew him well, I think he was happy all the time. I've known him by the thousands.'

'We had reached the last gate. Dusk drew around us and the town. I said: What has become of him now?'

From 'Return Journey' by Dylan Thomas

One of Swansea's most famous sons, Dylan Thomas, was born in Cwmdonkin Drive and raised in Uplands. He worked for the South Wales Evening Post, and Swansea was for him 'an ugly, lovely town, crawling, sprawling, slummed, unplanned, jerry-villaed and smug-suburbed by the side of a long and splendidly curving shore'. Thomas obviously had mixed feelings about his birthplace, but today's visitor can readily identify with these sentiments.

Lying on the west bank of the River Tawe, Swansea is also the gateway to the Gower Peninsula and has been described as the 'Brighton of Wales' (Gloucester Journal, 1786). For the workers and their families, to escape from Swansea's bustling industrial hothouse into the sanctuary of the beautiful Gower Peninsula must have been a real lifeline.

To the casual visitor, Swansea appears to be a very modern town, but it has a history stretching back many centuries. Its feeling of modernity is mostly attributable to the extensive rebuilding programmes of the 1950s and 1960s after the February 1941 blitz which laid waste much of Swansea. As a Channel port, it was an obvious target - docks, industry, flour mills and the large grain stores were considered vital to the war effort. The German High Command obviously agreed. Swansea was attacked forty-four times during the war, but the worst moments came on 19, 20 and 21 February 1941 when thousands of bombs and incendiaries were dropped on the town. These incendiaries caused the majority of the damage, claiming some notable victims, and the fires acted as a homing beacon for successive waves of German bombers to locate the town and deliver still more mayhem. The fires could be seen from as far away as Pembrokeshire and North Devon. The death toll was 230, with 400 injured. Much of

the city's architectural heritage was destroyed, and there are now only two remaining medieval buildings still surviving (the Castle and the Cross Keys Inn). It has to be said that the Victorian town planners also played their part by comprehensively demolishing entire streets to make way for developments.

The history of Swansea extends much further back than the Victorian era. Tradition has it that Sweyne Forkbeard, King of Denmark in 1013, settled here and gave the name of 'Sweyne's ey' to the immediate area ('ey' means inlet or islet). Old drawings do confirm that the River Tawe once divided to pass either side of a small islet in the mouth of the river. This would have made an excellent, easily defendable settlement.

The Normans also recognised its strategic importance. In 1106 Henry de Beaumont, Earl of Warwick and newly-appointed Lord of Gwyr or Gower, arrived; by 1116 he had built a castle on a small knoll near the river. This timber and turf structure was defended by a system of ditches and banks. De Beaumont was quite unpopular, and certainly needed to establish a fortress to consolidate his position. The Normans were the main catalyst for the growth of this frontier town in the shadow of its Castle. The Normans certainly did not have an easy time holding on to their conquests. In 1116 a Welsh army rampaged through Gower and attacked the Castle. They were fended off, but in 1192 the Castle was besieged for ten weeks. The experience was repeated in 1215 and 1217, but this time the Welsh attack was successful - the Castle was destroyed. 1257 and 1287 brought more attacks, which perhaps explains why William de Breos had started work on the 'New Castle', the remains of which we can see today. The River Tawe once flowed under its walls, but it was eventually rerouted to make way for the modern harbour and other developments. Much of the High Street and Wind Street and St Mary's Church would have been within the outer Castle wall.

During the Middle Ages the population of Swansea probably did not exceed 1,500, but it was still considered a major town in Wales. Its economy was based on agriculture and fishing; its trade was mainly local, but also reached as far afield as Ireland and Brittany. The fishermen, millers, saddlers and innkeepers gradually gave way as the demand for coal grew, and with it the introduction of copper smelting. There were many coalfields in the area, and the River Tawe was navigable far inland. The town burgeoned.

1712-20 there were 1,830 official inhabitants, but if the dissenters had been included, the total would probably have been more like 2,400. In 1717 the first copper works were established. The tempting combination of water, coal and iron ore were responsible for this. Swansea was once humorously referred to as 'Copperopolis'. In 1801 the first census gave the population as 6,099, and in 1848 Charles Cunliffe wrote: 'The Swansea Valley forms no bad representation of the infernal regions, for the smell aids the eye. Large groups of odd chimneys and rackety flues emit sulphurous, arsenical smoke or pure flame. A dense canopy overhangs the scene for several miles, rendered more horrible by the peculiar lurid glare. All vegetation is blasted in the valley and adjoining hills. On a clear day the smoke of the Swansea valley may be seen at a distance of forty or fifty miles and sometimes appears like a dense thundercloud'. By the 1880s, over 6,000 ships were visiting Swansea every year. Copper, zinc, steel and iron were all smelted in the town.

Perhaps it is due to its industrial heritage that Swansea's passion for open spaces and parks is

particularly felt. The Victorian 'aptitude for passionate reform' and the occasional sense of compassion for the 'sons of toil' fostered the drive to create recreational areas for the town. Once established, they became well-used as variously as can be imagined. The local militia would drill there, statues to local notables were raised, festivals and shows were held (from Buffalo Bill's Wild West Show to the National Eisteddfod). The parks worked their way into the civic and national pride of the town.

Timeline
some important dates in Swansea's history

c1013	Sweyne Forkbeard settles in the area.
1106	Henry de Beaumont, Earl of Warwick arrives.
1116	First castle is built. Population reaches c1,500.
1215/1217	Welsh destroy the castle.
1257	Welsh army attacks the city.
1287	Welsh army attacks the city.
1712-20	Population reaches 1,830, possibly actually as high as 2,400.
1717	First copper works established.
1801	First census gave the population as 6,099
1880s	Over 6,000 ships now visiting Swansea every year.
1941	The Blitz, when thousands of bombs and incendiaries were dropped on the city.
1950s/1960s	Extensive re-building programme.

General View 1893 32718
This picture of dense housing, factories, churches and civic
buildings nudging the port facilities of the North Dock illustrate
very well how the maritime economy was the lifeblood of the town.

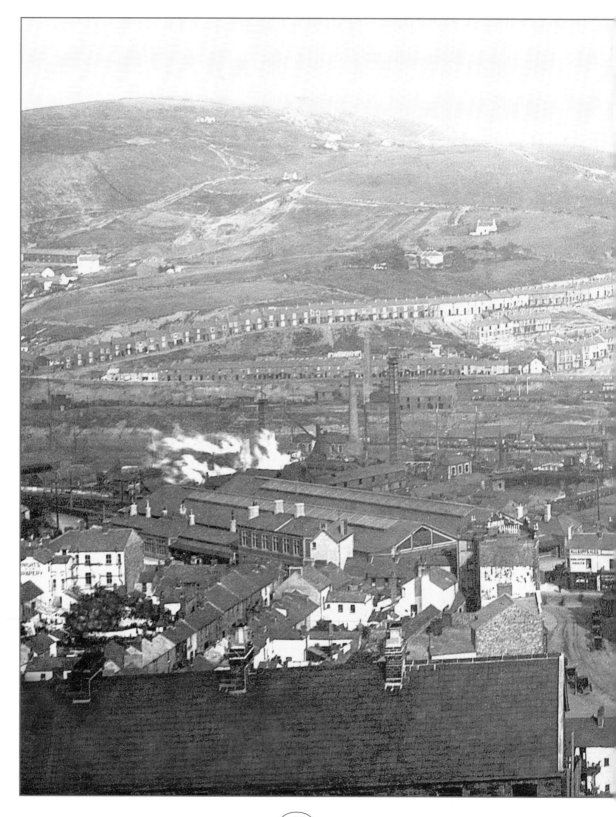

General View 1893
32719
This view looks out into the hills, which play such a part in defining Swansea. Notice the factory chimneys and their puff-ball smoky emissions. Sailing ships on the River Tawe and the long lines of terraced workers' cottages tell the tale of Swansea in its heyday as a major industrial town.

◀ **King's Dock 1893** 77356
When sail gave way to steam, a bigger dock was needed. All kinds of shipments left for destinations all over the world, with cargoes from copper ore and coal to potatoes and onions. The dock was named after King Edward VII; he and Queen Alexandra visited Swansea on 20 July 1904 to cut the first sod. Fully open in 1909, it was soon handling almost six million tonnes of goods per year. All this is now gone, and is presently the site of a superstore.

The Maritime Quarter

In 1722 the writer and traveller Daniel Defoe visited Swansea and commented: 'A very considerable town portrayed and has a very good harbour. There is also a very great trade for coal which they export to all the ports of Somerset, Devon and Cornwall and also to Ireland itself so that one sometimes sees a hundred sail of ships at a time loading coal here which greatly enriches the country and particularly the town of Swansea'. Swansea's maritime tradition has always been vital to the town, as can be seen from the many old drawings and paintings of the port, which all show large numbers of ships anchored in the Bay. The port, and the various extensions of it to accommodate ever bigger ships and greater volumes of cargo, drove the vigorous economic development of the town. The River Tawe used to run under the Castle walls until the port was enlarged by digging the New Cut for the river; thus the North Dock was created, which opened to traffic in the summer of 1852.

◄ **South Dock 1906** 54952

The South Dock opened in 1859, serving cargo vessels for regular services to London, Bristol, Liverpool, Dublin and Cork. The ship pictured here is the 'Talbot'. The shed survived the blitz, and now houses the Maritime Museum. Its gable end reads: 'Coast Lines Ltd. Sailings to and from all the principal ports of the United Kingdom. Shed 21'. The rail carriages linked the port facilities via a spur line to the GWR. network. It is now a marina.

◄ **Oil Tanker entering King's Dock 1925**

77366

The days of oil-fired ships, trains, power stations and the increasing demand for petrol meant that the importation of oil for the refineries had to be accommodated. This vessel is the 'British Consul' out of London.

The City Centre

Wind Street 1902 49003A
The name is pronounced 'Wine' Street; we are looking down towards the steel railway bridge. The 'New' Post Office is second on the left, and then Fitt Bros India Rubber and Asbestos Depot and the ornate gable end of the Adelphi Hotel. Circuses, including Barnum and Bailey's, once passed down here on their way to the Vetch field. The arrival of the overhead tram wires at the turn of the century put an end to this.

**Wind Street
and the Vivian Statue
1896** 38754
We are at the top of
Wind Street, once
home to this statue of
Sir Henry Hussey
Vivian, born in July
1821, created the first
Baron of Swansea in
1893, and died on 28
November 1894. The
Vivian family were
central to the
development of the
fortunes of the town.
The statue has been
relocated, and now
graces the precincts of
St Mary's Church.

◀ **St Mary's Church c1965**
S240249B
Here we see another reconstructed church, this time the responsibility of the Luftwaffe. The Victorian church was gutted in the 1941 blitz when its timber roof was destroyed by the incendiary bombs. The building was faithfully restored to its proper purpose between 1954-59 under the auspices of Sir Percy Thomas. On 28 May 1959, the new church was opened by Queen Elizabeth the Queen Mother.

St Mary's Church 1899 43668
The present building is the fifth church of this name to occupy the site. The nave collapsed in 1739, and was re-built on a much grander scale. It was re-built once more in 1895 on a still grander scale again.

St Mary's Church ▶ the Pulpit and the Organ c1965 S240243
The organ, by Norman and Beard, was installed in 1959 at a cost of £14,000. Originally in Woolwich Town Hall, this instrument has been well looked after and has enjoyed successive additions and refinements in 1976, 1988 and 1998.

◀ **St Mary's Church the Two Heads c1965**
S240247A
When the church was re-consecrated in May 1959, these two humorous carvings were put in place. They depict two war heroes: Winston Churchill, complete with characteristic hat and cigar on the left, and Montgomery on the right.

Castle Street 1925
77379
This view shows the ornate Ben Evans store in the distance. Note the F W Woolworth store on the left, and the tramlines in the road. The graceful arches of the Royal London Insurance offices are on the left behind the speeding motor car. The 'One shilling' sign is advertising lunches at R E Jones' Castle Cafe.

Castle Street 1925
77378
The 'new' castle buildings can be seen on the right. The offices of Royal London Insurance were once J W Evans' The Swansea Milliner; the building is now a Pizza Express. Note the R E Jones Castle Cafe, with its shilling lunches. Just past this was the Kardomah Cafe, made famous by Dylan Thomas and his associates, which was destroyed in the 1941 blitz.

◀ **The Castle Gardens c1965** S240235
The new David Evans store is on left; the original was destroyed in the 1941 blitz. The offices of the Swansea Evening Post are to the right. Now demolished, this building had variously been Town Hall, factory, jail, and post office. In its place there is now a paved area with sculpted water features.

◀ **The Castle 1893** 32724
What remains of the Castle buildings is now overshadowed by a glass, steel and concrete edifice to its rear. Built by the unpopular Norman Lord Henry de Beaufort in 1106, the Castle was his defence against the 'troublesome Welsh'. It did not, however, stop them from burning it to the ground in 1215 and 1217.

▼ **The Castle Gardens c1965** S240197
The Royal London Insurance offices are now Horsmith's, a car retailer for Daimler, Rover, Jaguar and Lanchester on its way to becoming a Pizza Express. The ornamental gardens are now gone.

◀ **Castle Square 1925**
77377
The striking Ben Evans store on the left was destroyed in the blitz of February 1941. The Midland Bank on the left is now, of course, a branch of HSBC. Note the decorators with their ladders stage left, the Halford's Cycle Co Ltd shop on the right; the Castle is just visible beyond, and the Vivian Statue is centre stage.

ALEXANDRA
RESTAURANT
AND
TEMPERANCE
HOTEL.

NESTLÉS
SWISS MILK
The Richest in Cream

32

High Street 1893
32720
Here we see the open-top trams of the High Street to Morriston and Cwmbwrla service. Notice the advertisement for Nestle Swiss Milk. Horse-drawn until the turn of the century, the trams provided much manure for Swansea gardeners. Notice the hand-cart on the left of the street.

High Street 1899 43975
Henry Chapman, Artist and Photographer advertises on the banner across the street and on the wall beyond the Alexandra. It is now an amusement arcade, but 'H Chapman' can still be seen above the portico. Note the advertisement for Fry's Cocoa on the tram. The Alexandra Restaurant and Temperance Hotel is now a Corel bookmakers!

High Street 1901 47956
The trams are now electric, having been switched over from horse-drawn in 1900. They were discontinued entirely in the late 1930s. The Hotel Cameron on the right was reconstructed in 1909 and became a branch of F W Woolworth in the 1930s. Note the 'Lucky Wedding Ring' sign on the left - an intriguing idea!

High Street 1910 62568
The new Hotel Cameron is on the right, having had its 1909 reconstruction. It was formerly a much humbler establishment, which only aspired to a second floor and was named the Hotel Cameron Arms. It had an inn yard in which customers' traps would be parked. It was damaged in the blitz, but largely survived. Note the Chappell's 30/- Suits advertisements further up the street.

▼ **Kingsway c1965** S240206
Mount Pleasant Baptist Church is on the right. The imposing concrete
street lights are now replaced by their less obvious modern
equivalents. The twin spires of St Andrew's Church can be dimly seen
in the distance. This road is considerably busier today!

▼ **The Library 1925** 77380
Situated in Alexandra Road, this magnificent building was opened by
William Gladstone in 1888.

▲ **The Grand Hotel c1965**
S240224
This building is opposite
the new railway station. It
is now very far indeed
from being in any way
'grand'; today it is a
motley collection of clubs
and bars.

◀ **The Dragon Hotel c1965**
S240226
This is a not-so-fine example of the reconstruction of Swansea that began in the 50s and 60s. Notice also the glorious lawns and flower beds situated in the centre of what would shortly become a busy roundabout. Were they to be enjoyed from a distance? Or to be glimpsed from a speeding car?

Craddock Street 1906
54946
The Albert Hall is on the right, which opened in 1864. It was once the most famous of Swansea's music halls. It had a variety of uses, but it was also a place of Sunday worship where the Rev Oscar Snelling would minister to his large flock. Notice the milk churns on the delivery cart to the left. Its original stone portico is now removed and today it is a Mecca Bingo Hall.

The Cliff Tram, Constitution Hill 1898 40920
The Constitution Hill Railway was constructed by the Incline Tramway Co, established in 1897. This feat of engineering was actually refused a Board of Trade certificate and was later abandoned.

Walter Road 1898 40921

We are looking along Walter Road in the direction of Uplands and Sketty. We have a good view of the Congregational Church, which is now no longer in existence.

Walter Road 1893 32723

After morning service many church- and chapel-goers would stroll along this tree-lined avenue. The Memorial Baptist Chapel is on the left; it is now completely rebuilt, very modern and very spire-less. In the distance we can see the spire of the Congregational Church. Notice the horse-drawn trap and the pedestrians in the road - the modern visitor would risk life and limb to do the same.

Walter Road 1906 54948
Taken thirteen years after No 32723, this view shows some interesting changes. The addition of tramlines and the
double-decker electric tram advertising the famous Ben Evans store would have been brought into service
sometime after the turn of the century. Notice also the girl with a hula-hoop on the right, two inquisitive boys and
a somewhat less inquisitive dog.

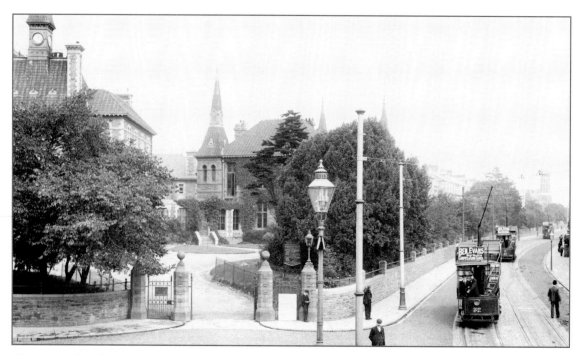

The General and Eye Hospital 1902 49002
We are on St Helen's Road, with St Andrew's Church just visible in the distance. The hospital was opened in 1869.
Here too, the electric tram advertises Ben Evans.

**The General
and Eye Hospital 1893** 32722
This image shows the same view as
49002 - only nine years earlier. There are
no overhead electric wires here and the
tram in the foreground is horsedrawn.

Oxford Street 1910

62566

Once the Carlton Cinema, the domed building is now a Waterstone's bookshop. The covered Victorian market to the right of the picture claimed to be the largest undercover market in Britain at the time. Built in 1897, and badly damaged in the 1941 three-night blitz of the city, it was itself a replacement for an even earlier market built in 1830.

The Guildhall 1906 54950
Built in the 1820s, and substantially altered in 1848, this building was variously the site of executions, a school, a courthouse and a venue for Swansea's Literature Festival. Most recently, it opened in 1995 as the Dylan Thomas Centre, with exhibition, conference centre, restaurant and bar facilities.

The Civic Buildings c1960 S240209
Designed by Sir Percy Thomas, the building was started in 1930 and was opened in 1934. Controversial at the time, it was representative of the modern movement in architecture, and is described as having a 'stripped classical' style.

The Civic Buildings c1960 S240119
Notice the prow of a Viking longboat in the clock-tower, a reminder of Sweyne Forkbeard and the city's Viking founders.

Swansea's Open Spaces

'As we were strolling on the sands we remarked a group of female figures in birthday attire gambolling in the water. In our subsequent rambles on the beach these liberal exhibitions of Cambrian beauty afforded us many pleasing studies of unsophisticated nature'.
J T Barber, 1803

Swansea was a hive of industry. Its Victorian patrons began to recognise the vital importance of recreation for the city's workforce and their families, but the 'liberal exhibitions' of the bathers in J T Barber's day would certainly not have been tolerated. The parks would often become venues for drilling the local militia, military band performances (the band members would camp out in the park), fetes, galas, May Day parades and shows. Churches also made use of the parks for open-air meetings and camps.

The Sands 1910 62573
This is the Slip, a popular meeting place and a place of recreation for so many years. The train track on the left is the Swansea Bay Station to Mumbles service. Notice the helter-skelter, the cycle roundabout, the stalls and other amusements.

▼ **The Sands 1925** 77372

Here we see Swansea Bay Station and the Slip. A fairground, market, ice-cream stalls, and so on were all to be found here in their day. The train and linking tram service here was a vital link for Swansea holidaymakers and Mumbles folk alike. The Bay View Hotel can be seen on the junction of St Helens Road and Oystermouth Road.

▼ **The Railway Station 1925** 77371

This is Swansea Bay Station, the terminus of the Mumbles Railway.

▲ **The Sands 1925** 77376
This view shows the Slip once again. The jetty to the waiting rowing boats was for pleasure trips.

◄ **Victoria Park 1902** 49003
These gardens opened on
21 June 1887 to
commemorate the Golden
Jubilee of Queen Victoria.
They are close to the new
civic buildings, and
meticulously maintained -
they must have been a joy
to see. They once
considerably exceeded their
present boundaries, but
have been much reduced
with time.

◄ **Victoria Park**
The Patti Pavilion
1925 77383
The Pavilion was built in 1920, five years before this photograph was taken, on the instructions of the famous Madame Patti, who had a mansion nearby. It was once home to the Welsh National Opera. The elaborate portico shown here has since been blocked in to frustrate vandals and deter the homeless from taking up residence.

Victoria Park
The Floral Clock 1925
77381
The site of this elaborate timepiece is now built over, but the author is given to understand that the mechanism was rescued and is at present in storage.

Brynmill Park 1925
77384
This is the 'Swan Park'. As 19th-century Swansea outgrew its water supply, the Board of Health remedied the situation by building two reservoirs, one at Brynmill and one at Cwmdonkin. Brynmill reservoir was opened in 1839, and was once much bigger than it is today.

Brynmill Park 1925
77385
In July 1905, the National Lifeboat Association held a demonstration on the lake. Good Friday and Easter Monday would see a miniature fair - stalls for refreshments, model yacht racing on the reservoir, rowing boats for hire, bowls and so on.

▼ **Brynmill Park 1925** 77386
Here we see the 'tropical island' and the lodge.

▼ **Cwmdonkin Park 1896** 38756
This was a place of many memories for Dylan Thomas, who was born near here. The reservoir was open by 1880; to avoid the surplus land thereabouts being built on (and thereby possibly contaminating the reservoir), it was decided to create a park, and 'to set the land out as a public boon' (notice in the Cambrian, 1871).

▲ **Cwmdonkin Park 1925**
77387
The 1907 Eisteddfod Gorsedd ceremonies were held here. A favourite destination for the upper classes after Sunday Chapel and Church services.

◄ From the Railway Bridge 1898 40918
Cricket had been played in Swansea since the 18th century, and Swansea folk have always been passionate about their sport. Note the pavilion on the opposite side of the field, and the groundsman who can be dimly seen tending the pitch.

The Outlying Areas

Swansea in its industrial heyday was a vigorous, sprawling giant. Outlying villages and townships were absorbed into the expanding city, which even gave rise to the very existence of some of them.

Llansamlet, Heol Las 1938 88274
This parish is within Swansea's industrial catchment area; it overlooks the Tawe valley. It was built principally on its tin-plate and spelter works.

Llansamlet, Heol Las 1938 88275
Although the area developed rapidly in the 19th century (the population was 3,375 in 1841 and increased to 9,721 in 1891), it has been a settlement for much longer. The parish of Llansamlet derives its name from the 7th-century St Samlet, and Llansamlet simply means 'Samlet's town' or 'enclosure'.

Sketty, St Paul's Church 1896 38763
Built by the Vivian family of Singleton Abbey in 1850, this tranquil image has changed very little, except for the addition of several more recent parts to the Church.

Sketty, St Paul's Church 1910 62584
Once a sleepy village far removed from the hustle and bustle of its neighbour by green fields, Sketty is now very much part of the extended city of Swansea. Between the wars, the urban sprawl of the city engulfed the village, and developments pushed west and north from the city centre.

**Morriston
Woodfield Street
c1955** M179033
The distinctive
Tabernacle
Congregational Chapel
is on the right. The town
had its origins in the
rapid outward
commercial expansion
of the industry from the
centre of Swansea. Note
the F W Woolworth
store on the right.

◀ **Morriston**
The Cross c1955
M179037

◄ **Morriston, Woodfield Street c1955** M179017
Note the branch of John Lewis, Complete Outfitters on the right, and the Regal Cinema on the left.

▼ **Clydach, The Lower Fall 1893** 32603
Despite its industrial heritage, spectacular scenery is never very far away from the city.

◄ **Skewen, The Arches 1937** 87892

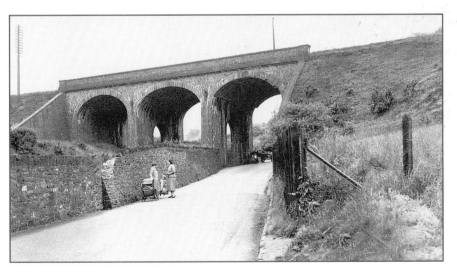

▼ **Skewen, General View 1937** 87895

▼ **Gowerton, Sterry Road c1955** G152002
The village of Gowerton, or Tre-Gwyr, was once the heart of a busy coal-field, which is now, of course, no longer in existence.

▲ **Gowerton, The Afon Llan Navigation c1955**
G152007
By this time popular with pleasure boats, the Afon Llan navigation would once have been vital to the commercial success of the village; it was used for transporting coal from here to Penclawdd.

◄ **Gowerton c1955** G152003
Messing about in boats has
always been a timeless
pursuit. The image
portrayed here gives no
clue to the industrial roots
of this area, which were
mainly based around coal
and the smelting of iron,
copper, zinc and tin. The
navigation here would have
been vital, and the rapid
development of the road,
canal and rail systems was
driven by these industries.

Gowerton c1955 G152004

Gorseinon, St Catherine's Church 1936 87815
Eglwys Santes Catrin to the Welsh, this magnificent building dedicated to St Catherine looks over the centre of the town. The urban development of Swansea between the two World Wars massively increased the population of areas such as Gorseinon, which practically sprang up out of open countryside.

Gorseinon, The Square 1936 87814
Now a charity shop, 'Peglers' on the right is still identifiable as the name can still be clearly seen in the doorway.

Pontarddulais
Swansea Road c1955 P165018
The Dulais Pharmacy, Gwyn Jones, Dispensing Chemist is on the
right before the Chapel. Lloyds Bank is further up on the right.

Pontarddulais, The Viaduct c1955 P165004
Another vital link in the industrial network of the area, the viaduct helped to transport the coal and thereby service the iron, copper, zinc and tin industries of the area.

Pontlliw, Gwynn's Service Station 1937 87906

Points East

It was some time before the industrialists of Swansea recognised the potential for development east of the River Tawe. The extension of the docks in that area was even a matter of some controversy, but in time reliable, rapid communications were built which inspired the growth of the townships in that direction. The key to it all was, of course, the bridges.

Swansea, The New Bridge c1960 S240200
This was a major link for points east for the city. The first bridge across the River Tawe was opened in 1852 on the site of the present Sainsbury's supermarket. Before this, the only way across was by ferryboat, a dangerous business - people were occasionally drowned. Long gone are the days of the Ha'Penny Bridge and Pottery Bridge, when tolls were payable to get across the river.

**Neath, Green Street
1898** 40953
The row of shops on
the right advertise 'Hot
& Cold Baths and
Billiards', 'Eastman's
Meat Purveyors', and
'Rees Clothier and
Outfitter'. The Globe
Cinema can be seen
further down.

▼ **Neath, The Abbey 1893** 32725A

Set on the banks of the Tennant Canal, the Abbey was founded in 1130 by the Norman baron Richard de Granville. John Leland in the 16th century described the abbey as 'the fairest in all Wales'. After it was dissolved in 1539, the abbey was partly converted into a mansion; after a spell as a copper smelting and casting factory, it has now been preserved by CADW.

▼ **Neath, Victoria Gardens 1898** 40946B

Note the essential bandstand and the lady sitting with her canopied pram.

▲ **Briton Ferry
The New Bridge c1965**

B398017

The M4 motorway is South Wales's arterial route to the south of England, connecting South Wales as far as Carmarthen with London. As well as servicing the industrial heartland of Neath, Port Talbot and Swansea, it also forms a vital link for the mainly agricultural areas of South and West Wales.

◀ **Briton Ferry**
The New Bridge c1965
B398019
This sea-port at the mouth
of the Nedd derived its
importance from its docks
and from its steel and
tin works.

◀ **Port Talbot
The M4 Motorway
c1960** P139063
The building of the M4
created vast numbers of
jobs, and the road
continues to sustain
those that remain
working in local industry.
Without this vital link to
the rest of Britain, their
future would surely be
even less secure than it
is at present, so we must
forgive the car fumes
and noise.

Port Talbot, Station Road c1955 P139021

Originally part of the ancient borough of Aberafan, Welsh for 'the mouth of the river', Port Talbot was once a thriving industrial town built on steel, coal-mining and tin plate manufacturing. What remains of this is much reduced in size and output.

Margam, The Park and Mynydd 1938 88303

Margam, with its abbey, was a centre of Christian worship for over 1,000 years from the time when monks of the Celtic church established a monastery here. Robert de Gloucester founded a Cistercian monastery here in 1147; its grounds are now mostly occupied by the mansion house, but the choir and the chapter house remain.

Margam The Round Chapel 1938 88302

This is now the site of part of the M4 motorway, but the Chapel itself has been re-located. Mansell Talbot gave permission for the sale of the land to the Church, subject to them providing a design which met his approval. This building is modelled on a church in Switzerland.

Margam Castle 1936 87738

Built by Mansell Talbot at the beginning of the 19th century in part of the Margam Abbey grounds, this splendid building subsequently went into decline until it was taken over by the Council and restored. The Mansell family acquired Margam in the 16th century, and the south aisle of the abbey contains family tombs.

Margam Castle c1955 P139001

Points West

In complete contrast to the industrial heartland of Port Talbot, heading west we find the glorious, unspoilt beauty of the Gower Peninsula, which stretches for 20km into the Bristol Channel. Rich in monuments and relics, the Gower has drawn large numbers of visitors for centuries; it was the first designated Area of Outstanding Natural Beauty.

Mumbles
From the Quarry 1893 32726
Clement's Quarry is in the foreground. Note the area of tidal reach between the railtracks. The Mumbles-Swansea train in the centre is heading for or leaving the Elms Terminus. Bank Holidays would see upwards of 3,000 passengers per train; 40,000 to 50,000 people would travel to Mumbles on the busiest days of the year.

◄ **Mumbles**
General View 1925
77402
Note that the area of
tidal reach is now built
over. The cinema, centre
right, is the Tivoli; it was
formerly known as the
Kursaal. It is now an
amusement arcade. The
gable end of the shop
visible in the centre
reads 'J Bailey,
Family Butcher'.

◄ Blackpill 'Roman' Bridge 1893

32740

This is not, in fact a Roman bridge at all, but was probably built in the 18th century. This fact could be slightly awkward for Roman Court and Roman Bridge Lane, two newly-built housing developments nearby. The bridge is now the subject of controversy: it is scheduled for relocation to make way for a leisure centre.

▼ Mumbles Oystermouth Castle c1960 M108004

The ivy-clad castle is approached via Castle Avenue. 'Oystermouth Castle is a majestic ruin, in a bold situation near the sea coast, commanding a delightful prospect of the country, and surrounded by broken cliffs'. (Benjamin Malkin, c1803).

◄ Mumbles, Oystermouth Castle 1893 32739

This is one of the most intact castles in Gower; it has all of the features castle enthusiasts will enjoy. It was variously occupied and controlled by Norman barons and Welsh princes, including Owain Glyndwr. 'There is in this parish a very spacious castle having many dry Roomes, vaults and sellers in it, with staires, towers and walkes very firm, in some arches there are flowers and coates of arms painted in divers colours'. (Isaac Hamon, 1690s).

Mumbles, The Promenade 1898 40928
This former humble fishing village achieved an enviable reputation as a holiday destination in the 18th century, which it has retained. The Marine Hotel can be seen in the distance, and the shop sign on the extreme left reads 'R S Skinner - Baker, Confectioner'.

Mumbles, The Promenade 1898 40927
This is Promenade Terrace and Parade Gardens (the area reclaimed from the sea). On the left we can see 'James Webborn, Tea & Coffee, Oysters, Refreshments, Carriages for Hire', the decorator at work on his ladder, and the Dining Rooms.

Mumbles
Southend 1925 77405
We are looking towards Mumbles
Head. The Ship and Castle public
house is now the Conservative Club.

**Mumbles
The Pier 1898** 40925
Here we see the terminus of the Swansea to
Mumbles railway. The pier was essential for the
recreation of Edwardian visitors to this part of
the seaside. The pier was also the embarkation
point for paddle steamers. Note the sailing
ships in the Channel, and the steam train. The
carriage advertises 'Liptons Teas -
largest sale in the world'.

Mumbles, The Lighthouse 1893 32731
This picture of the famous lighthouse on Middle Head was taken from Bracelet Bay. Built in 1794, the lighthouse originally had two platforms, each with a coal-fired beacon to warn shipping of the dangers of the Mixon Sands and Cherry Stone Rock. In 1799 it became oil-fired, and it was converted to electricity in 1905. The last keeper retired in 1934 when it became an automatic light; it is presently the responsibility of Trinity House.

Mumbles, The Lighthouse 1925 77404
This view was taken from Limeslade Bay, looking over the Tutt on the road cut in 1887 to connect the main road to Bracelet and Limeslade.

Parkmill, The Gower Hotel 1910 62589
This was a popular coaching inn; it has since been renamed the Gower Inn to reflect its new-found function as a public house. The attractive building in the centre is the former school, now the West Glamorgan Guides Activity Centre. Further down the road we come to the Gower Heritage Centre.

Parkmill, The Village 1893 32756
The bridge over the Ilston River can still be found, although the river is much reduced. The walk up the Ilston valley to Ilston Church is picturesque. John Wesley's pulpit can be found half a mile up the valley.

Index

Frith Book Co Titles

www.frithbook.co.uk

The Frith Book Company publishes over 100 new titles each year. A selection of those currently available are listed below. For latest catalogue please contact Frith Book Co.

Town Books 96pp, 100 photos. County and Themed Books 128pp, 150 photos (unless specified). All titles hardback laminated case and jacket except those indicated pb (paperback)

Around Bakewell	1-85937-113-2	£12.99	Around Great Yarmouth	1-85937-085-3	£12.99
Around Barnstaple	1-85937-084-5	£12.99	Around Guildford	1-85937-117-5	£12.99
Around Bath	1-85937-097-7	£12.99	Hampshire	1-85937-064-0	£14.99
Berkshire (pb)	1-85937-191-4	£9.99	Around Harrogate	1-85937-112-4	£12.99
Around Blackpool	1-85937-049-7	£12.99	Around Horsham	1-85937-127-2	£12.99
Around Bognor Regis	1-85937-055-1	£12.99	Around Ipswich	1-85937-133-7	£12.99
Around Bournemouth	1-85937-067-5	£12.99	Ireland (pb)	1-85937-181-7	£9.99
Brighton (pb)	1-85937-192-2	£8.99	Isle of Man	1-85937-065-9	£14.99
British Life A Century Ago	1-85937-103-5	£17.99	Isle of Wight	1-85937-114-0	£14.99
Buckinghamshire (pb)	1-85937-200-7	£9.99	Kent (pb)	1-85937-189-2	£9.99
Around Cambridge	1-85937-092-6	£12.99	Around Leicester	1-85937-073-x	£12.99
Cambridgeshire	1-85937-086-1	£14.99	Leicestershire (pb)	1-85937-185-x	£9.99
Canals and Waterways	1-85937-129-9	£17.99	Around Lincoln	1-85937-111-6	£12.99
Cheshire	1-85937-045-4	£14.99	Lincolnshire	1-85937-135-3	£14.99
Around Chester	1-85937-090-x	£12.99	London (pb)	1-85937-183-3	£9.99
Around Chichester	1-85937-089-6	£12.99	Around Maidstone	1-85937-056-x	£12.99
Churches of Berkshire	1-85937-170-1	£17.99	New Forest	1-85937-128-0	£14.99
Churches of Dorset	1-85937-172-8	£17.99	Around Newark	1-85937-105-1	£12.99
Colchester (pb)	1-85937-188-4	£8.99	Around Newquay	1-85937-140-x	£12.99
Cornwall	1-85937-054-3	£14.99	North Devon Coast	1-85937-146-9	£14.99
Cumbria	1-85937-101-9	£14.99	Northumberland and Tyne & Wear		
Dartmoor	1-85937-145-0	£14.99		1-85937-072-1	£14.99
Around Derby	1-85937-046-2	£12.99	Norwich (pb)	1-85937-194-9	£8.99
Derbyshire (pb)	1-85937-196-5	£9.99	Around Nottingham	1-85937-060-8	£12.99
Devon	1-85937-052-7	£14.99	Nottinghamshire (pb)	1-85937-187-6	£9.99
Dorset	1-85937-075-6	£14.99	Around Oxford	1-85937-096-9	£12.99
Dorset Coast	1-85937-062-4	£14.99	Oxfordshire	1-85937-076-4	£14.99
Down the Severn	1-85937-118-3	£14.99	Peak District	1-85937-100-0	£14.99
Down the Thames	1-85937-121-3	£14.99	Around Penzance	1-85937-069-1	£12.99
Around Dublin	1-85937-058-6	£12.99	Around Plymouth	1-85937-119-1	£12.99
East Sussex	1-85937-130-2	£14.99	Around St Ives	1-85937-068-3	£12.99
Around Eastbourne	1-85937-061-6	£12.99	Around Scarborough	1-85937-104-3	£12.99
Edinburgh (pb)	1-85937-193-0	£8.99	Scotland (pb)	1-85937-182-5	£9.99
English Castles	1-85937-078-0	£14.99	Scottish Castles	1-85937-077-2	£14.99
Essex	1-85937-082-9	£14.99	Around Sevenoaks and Tonbridge		
Around Exeter	1-85937-126-4	£12.99		1-85937-057-8	£12.99
Exmoor	1-85937-132-9	£14.99	Around Southampton	1-85937-088-8	£12.99
Around Falmouth	1-85937-066-7	£12.99	Around Southport	1-85937-106-x	£12.99

Available from your local bookshop or from the publisher

Frith Book Co Titles (continued)

Around Shrewsbury	1-85937-110-8	£12.99
Shropshire	1-85937-083-7	£14.99
South Devon Coast	1-85937-107-8	£14.99
South Devon Living Memories		
	1-85937-168-x	£14.99
Staffordshire (96pp)	1-85937-047-0	£12.99
Stone Circles & Ancient Monuments		
	1-85937-143-4	£17.99
Around Stratford upon Avon		
	1-85937-098-5	£12.99
Sussex (pb)	1-85937-184-1	£9.99

Around Torbay	1-85937-063-2	£12.99
Around Truro	1-85937-147-7	£12.99
Victorian & Edwardian Kent		
	1-85937-149-3	£14.99
Victorian & Edwardian Yorkshire		
	1-85937-154-x	£14.99
Warwickshire (pb)	1-85937-203-1	£9.99
Welsh Castles	1-85937-120-5	£14.99
West Midlands	1-85937-109-4	£14.99
West Sussex	1-85937-148-5	£14.99
Wiltshire	1-85937-053-5	£14.99
Around Winchester	1-85937-139-6	£12.99

Frith Book Co titles available Autumn 2000

Croydon Living Memories (pb)			
	1-85937-162-0	£9.99	Aug
Glasgow (pb)	1-85937-190-6	£9.99	Aug
Hertfordshire (pb)	1-85937-247-3	£9.99	Aug
North London	1-85937-206-6	£14.99	Aug
Victorian & Edwardian Maritime Album			
	1-85937-144-2	£17.99	Aug
Victorian Seaside	1-85937-159-0	£17.99	Aug
Cornish Coast	1-85937-163-9	£14.99	Sep
County Durham	1-85937-123-x	£14.99	Sep
Dorset Living Memories	1-85937-210-4	£14.99	Sep
Herefordshire	1-85937-174-4	£14.99	Sep
Kent Living Memories	1-85937-125-6	£14.99	Sep
Leeds (pb)	1-85937-202-3	£9.99	Sep
Ludlow (pb)	1-85937-176-0	£9.99	Sep
Norfolk (pb)	1-85937-195-7	£9.99	Sep
Somerset	1-85937-153-1	£14.99	Sep
Tees Valley & Cleveland	1-85937-211-2	£14.99	Sep
Thanet (pb)	1-85937-116-7	£9.99	Sep
Tiverton (pb)	1-85937-178-7	£9.99	Sep
Victorian and Edwardian Sussex			
	1-85937-157-4	£14.99	Sep

Weymouth (pb)	1-85937-209-0	£9.99	Sep
Worcestershire	1-85937-152-3	£14.99	Sep
Yorkshire Living Memories	1-85937-166-3	£14.99	Sep
British Life A Century Ago (pb)			
	1-85937-213-9	£9.99	Oct
Camberley (pb)	1-85937-222-8	£9.99	Oct
Cardiff (pb)	1-85937-093-4	£9.99	Oct
Carmarthenshire	1-85937-216-3	£14.99	Oct
Cornwall (pb)	1-85937-229-5	£9.99	Oct
English Country Houses	1-85937-161-2	£17.99	Oct
Humberside	1-85937-215-5	£14.99	Oct
Manchester (pb)	1-85937-198-1	£9.99	Oct
Middlesex	1-85937-158-2	£14.99	Oct
Norfolk Living Memories	1-85937-217-1	£14.99	Oct
Preston (pb)	1-85937-212-0	£9.99	Oct
South Hams	1-85937-220-1	£14.99	Oct
Suffolk	1-85937-221-x	£9.99	Oct
Swansea (pb)	1-85937-167-1	£9.99	Oct
West Yorkshire (pb)	1-85937-201-5	£9.99	Oct

See Frith books on the internet www.frithbook.co.uk

FRITH PRODUCTS & SERVICES

Francis Frith would doubtless be pleased to know that the pioneering publishing venture he started in 1860 still continues today. A hundred and forty years later, The Francis Frith Collection continues in the same innovative tradition and is now one of the foremost publishers of vintage photographs in the world. Some of the current activities include:

Interior Decoration

Today Frith's photographs can be seen framed and as giant wall murals in thousands of pubs, restaurants, hotels, banks, retail stores and other public buildings throughout the country. In every case they enhance the unique local atmosphere of the places they depict and provide reminders of gentler days in an increasingly busy and frenetic world.

Product Promotions

Frith products are used by many major companies to promote the sales of their own products or to reinforce their own history and heritage. Frith promotions have been used by Hovis bread, Courage beers, Scots Porage Oats, Colman's mustard, Cadbury's foods, Mellow Birds coffee, Dunhill pipe tobacco, Guinness, and Bulmer's Cider.

Genealogy and Family History

As the interest in family history and roots grows world-wide, more and more people are turning to Frith's photographs of Great Britain for images of the towns, villages and streets where their ancestors lived; and, of course, photographs of the churches and chapels where their ancestors were christened, married and buried are an essential part of every genealogy tree and family album.

Frith Products

All Frith photographs are available Framed or just as Mounted Prints and Posters (size 23 x 16 inches). These may be ordered from the address below. From time to time other products - Address Books, Calendars, Table Mats, etc - are available.

The Internet

Already twenty thousand Frith photographs can be viewed and purchased on the internet. By the end of the year 2000 some 60,000 Frith photographs will be available on the internet. The number of sites is constantly expanding, each focussing on different products and services from the Collection.
The main Frith sites are listed below.

www.francisfrith.co.uk
www.frithbook.co.uk

See the complete list of Frith Books at:

www.frithbook.co.uk

This web site is regularly updated with the latest list of publications from the Frith Book Company. If you wish to buy books relating to another part of the country that your local bookshop does not stock, you may purchase on-line.

For further information, trade, or author enquiries please contact us at the address below:
The Francis Frith Collection, Frith's Barn, Teffont, Salisbury, Wiltshire, England SP3 5QP.
Tel: +44 (0)1722 716 376 Fax: +44 (0)1722 716 881   Email: uksales@francisfrith.com

See Frith books on the internet www.frithbook.co.uk

TO RECEIVE YOUR FREE MOUNTED PRINT

Mounted Print
Overall size 14 x 11 inches

Cut out this Voucher and return it with your remittance for £1.50 to cover postage and handling, to UK addresses. For overseas addresses please include £4.00 post and handling. Choose any photograph included in this book. Your SEPIA print will be A4 in size, and mounted in a cream mount with burgundy rule lines, overall size 14 x 11 inches.

Order additional Mounted Prints at HALF PRICE (only £7.49 each*)

If there are further pictures you would like to order, possibly as gifts for friends and family, purchase them at half price (no additional postage and handling required).

Have your Mounted Prints framed*

For an additional £14.95 per print you can have your chosen Mounted Print framed in an elegant polished wood and gilt moulding, overall size 16 x 13 inches (no additional postage and handling required).

---

* IMPORTANT!
These special prices are only available if ordered using the original voucher on this page (no copies permitted) and at the same time as your free Mounted Print, for delivery to the same address

---

Frith Collectors' Guild

From time to time we publish a magazine of news and stories about Frith photographs and further special offers of Frith products. If you would like 12 months FREE membership, please return this form.

Send completed forms to:
The Francis Frith Collection, Frith's Barn, Teffont, Salisbury, Wiltshire SP3 5QP

$\mathscr{V}\!oucher$ for **FREE** and Reduced Price Frith Prints

Picture no.	Page number	Qty	Mounted @ £7.49	Framed + £14.95	Total Cost
		1	**Free of charge***	£	£
			£7.49	£	£
			£7.49	£	£
			£7.49	£	£
			£7.49	£	£
			£7.49	£	£

Please allow 28 days for delivery	*** Post & handling**	**£1.50**
Book Title	**Total Order Cost**	**£**

Please do not photocopy this voucher. Only the original is valid, so please cut it out and return it to us.

I enclose a cheque / postal order for £ . . . .
made payable to 'The Francis Frith Collection'
OR please debit my Mastercard / Visa / Switch / Amex card

Number . . . .

Issue No(Switch only) . . . . .Valid from (Amex/Switch) . . . .

Expires . . . . Signature . . . .

Name Mr/Mrs/Ms . . . .

Address . . . .

. . . .

. . . .

. . . . Postcode . . . .

Daytime Tel No . . . .   Valid to 31/12/02

The Francis Frith Collectors' Guild

Please enrol me as a member for 12 months free of charge.

Name Mr/Mrs/Ms . . . .

Address . . . .

. . . .

. . . .

. . . . Postcode . . . .

Free Print - see overleaf